POINTS OF VIEW

Should the MINIMUM WAGE Be Raised?

By Layla Owens

KidHaven
PUBLISHING

Published in 2023 by
KidHaven Publishing, an Imprint of Greenhaven Publishing, LLC
29 E. 21st Street
New York, NY 10010

Designer: Deanna Paternostro
Editor: Caitie McAneney

Photo credits: Cover BlueSkyImage/Shutterstock.com; p. 5 Altrendo Images/Shutterstock.com; p. 7 kitzcorner/Shutterstock.com; p. 9 Frederic Legrand - COMEO/Shutterstock.com; p. 11 Dmytro Zinkevych/Shutterstock.com; p. 13 Africa Studio/Shutterstock.com; p. 15 kormakova1/Shuterstock.com; p. 17 LightField Studios/Shutterstock.com; p. 19 Prostock-studio/Shutterstock.com; p. 21 (notepad) ESB Professional/Shutterstock.com; p. 21 (markers) Kucher Serhii/Shutterstock.com; p. 21 (photo frame) FARBAI/iStock/Thinkstock; p. 21 (inset, left) Paul Vasarhelyi/Shutterstock.com; p. 21 (inset, middle) a katz/Shutterstock.com; p. 21 (inset, right) Damir Khabirov/Shutterstock.com.

Library of Congress Cataloging-in-Publication Data

Names: Owens, Layla, author.
Title: Should the minimum wage be raised? / Layla Owens.
Description: New York : KidHaven Publishing, [2023] | Series: Points of view | Includes index.
Identifiers: LCCN 2021050976 (print) | LCCN 2021050977 (ebook) | ISBN 9781534542037 (library binding) | ISBN 9781534542013 (paperback) | ISBN 9781534542020 (set) | ISBN 9781534542044 (ebook)
Subjects: LCSH: Minimum wage–United States–Juvenile literature. | Living wage movement–United States–Juvenile literature.
Classification: LCC HD4918 .O94 2023 (print) | LCC HD4918 (ebook) | DDC 331.2/30973–dc23/eng/20211025
LC record available at https://lccn.loc.gov/2021050976
LC ebook record available at https://lccn.loc.gov/2021050977

Printed in the United States of America

CPSIA compliance information: Batch #CSKH23: For further information contact Greenhaven Publishing LLC, New York, New York at 1-844-317-7404.

CONTENTS

A Fair WAGE

As a kid, you might not think too much about the minimum wage. That's the lowest amount of money an **employer** can pay their workers. However, it's an important issue in the United States today that affects many people. Many Americans are calling for raising the minimum wage to at least $15 an hour.

Many people argue that the minimum wage needs to be higher to fight **poverty**. Other people say raising the minimum wage would hurt business and cost people their jobs. You can look at both sides of this **debate** to form your own opinion.

Know the Facts!

In 1938, the Fair Labor Standards Act created the first **federal** minimum wage in the United States.

People use their wages to pay for food, housing, clothes, and more.

What Is Minimum WAGE?

The first federal minimum wage was only $0.25 an hour in 1938. Over time, the minimum wage increased as more goods and services were produced or to keep up with **inflation**.

Today, the federal minimum wage is $7.25 an hour, as of 2021. Each state has different minimum wages, though. Some states like Texas set their minimum wage at $7.25 an hour, while other states like California set minimum wages above $13 an hour. In addition, people who earn tips at work, such as workers at restaurants, can be paid less than the minimum wage, and full-time students can be paid less at some jobs too.

Know the Facts!

The COVID-19 **pandemic** led to lost jobs as well as inflation, causing hardship for many Americans.

Some people argue that the minimum wage has not kept up with inflation, so people can't afford to buy as much as in years past.

The Poverty PROBLEM

In 2018, 38.1 million people in the United States were living in poverty. That's nearly 12 percent of the total population. Many people living in poverty have at least one job. Some people have to work two jobs or many extra hours to afford what they need to live.

Some people argue that much of the poverty problem comes from a low minimum wage. They think that if the minimum wage were raised, workers would be able to afford what they need, such as housing and food. They think it's wrong when the people who own businesses get richer while their workers stay in poverty.

Know the Facts!

In January 2021, the Congressional Budget Office (CBO) stated that a wage increase to $15 an hour could lift 1 million people out of poverty.

People think that businesses should share their **profits** with all their workers to keep them out of poverty.

Bad for BUSINESS

Businesses need to make a profit to stay open. A business's income is the money that comes in from the goods and services it sells. Then, the business spends money on **materials** and paying employees. The money left over after that money is spent is the profit.

People who are against raising the minimum wage argue that it would be bad for businesses. Larger companies might be able to afford to pay their workers $15 an hour because they make a lot of profit. However, smaller businesses might not be able to make a profit if the minimum wage is raised.

Know the Facts!

A 2021 CNBC poll of small businesses showed that 54 percent were against raising the minimum wage.

Some small businesses are owned by families. They may not be able to stay open if they have to pay their employees a higher minimum wage.

Raising the RENT

Some people rent their apartment or house. That means someone else owns it and they pay rent to live there. Rent has been rising greatly across the United States each year, even as the minimum wage stays the same or increases only slightly.

People argue that the minimum wage should rise so people can pay the rising cost of rent. Rental costs are higher than the income from the hourly minimum wage in every state in the United States as of 2021. If a person can't pay their rent, they can be kicked out of their home. Then, they could be homeless.

Know the Facts!

On average, a person would need to earn $24.90 per hour for a 40-hour workweek to afford a two-bedroom rental property in the United States.

About 25 percent of the homeless population in the United States has at least one job.

Jobs at RISK

Many people would rather keep their job, even at a lower wage, than lose their job. Some argue that people will lose their jobs if the minimum wage is raised. Employers would cut jobs to afford to pay the new wage. Some businesses may even have to close. Then, all of their workers would be out of their jobs.

People who oppose raising the minimum wage argue that people should work more hours or pick up a second job to make enough money. These people want to **protect** jobs, especially after many people lost their jobs during the COVID-19 pandemic.

Know the Facts!

The CBO has said that 1.4 million people could lose their jobs if the minimum wage is raised to $15 an hour.

People depend on jobs for income, as well as **benefits** such as health care.

Purchasing POWER

Purchasing power is the amount of goods or services you can buy. Purchasing power has gone down in recent decades. That means a person can buy less with their money than they used to. The minimum wage is growing more slowly than the price of goods and services.

One example is buying a house. In 1965, the average price for a new home in the United States was $21,000. However, in 2021, the average price was $408,800. Wages haven't risen enough to cover this difference. Many people put off making big purchases because they don't have the purchasing power.

Know the Facts!

A 2019 report showed that the purchasing power of someone making minimum wage had gone down 31 percent since 1968.

Many argue that wages need to increase so people can afford basic needs, like food, as well as big purchases.

Price INCREASES

Many people think that raising the minimum wage will lead to worse inflation. They say that businesses will have to raise the prices for their goods and services to make up for profits lost to increased wages.

Some people give the example of a fast-food restaurant. The food is cheap because many fast-food restaurants pay their workers minimum wage. If the restaurant has to pay workers $15 an hour, they'll have to charge **consumers** more for their food. Then, people's purchasing power will once again go down.

Know the Facts!

People **calculate** inflation by looking at the yearly change in the consumer price index (CPI). The CPI looks at prices paid by consumers for certain goods over time.

Dealing with increased prices for goods makes it hard for people to afford what they need.

A Living WAGE

The federal minimum wage has changed many times since it was first created. In many cases, these increases have been met with strong opinions both for and against higher wages.

Many Americans believe the minimum wage should be raised to $15 an hour. They say it would decrease the **wealth gap** between the lower and middle classes and the wealth gap between races. It would ensure a living wage, or enough money to meet basic needs. Others don't want the minimum wage raised or say that it can be raised—just not up to $15 an hour. What's your point of view?

Know the Facts!

More than 60 percent of U.S. adults want to raise the federal minimum wage to $15 an hour.

Should the minimum wage be raised?

YES

- It would help people out of poverty.
- Rent is increasing, so wages should increase too.
- If people have more money, then they'll spend more money.
- It would help decrease the wealth gap between lower and middle classes.

NO

- It would put companies out of business.
- It could cost people their jobs.
- It could increase prices of goods and services.
- An increase to $15 an hour is too high to make all at once.

You can share an informed, or educated, opinion about this debate using this chart to help you.

GLOSSARY

benefit: A good or service received.

calculate: To find the solution to a problem using math processes.

consumer: A person who has purchased goods or services.

debate: An argument or discussion about an issue, generally between two sides.

employer: A person or company that provides a job paying wages or a salary to one or more people.

federal: Relating to the central government of the United States.

inflation: A continuing rise in the price of things.

material: Something from which something else can be made.

pandemic: An outbreak of disease that occurs over a wide geographic area and affects a great proportion of the population.

poverty: The state of being poor.

profit: Money that is made.

protect: To keep safe.

wealth gap: The difference in earnings between two groups.

For More INFORMATION

WEBSITES

5 Things Kids Need to Know About Coronavirus
www.hopkinsmedicine.org/health/conditions-and-diseases/coronavirus/5-things-kids-need-to-know-about-coronavirus
COVID-19 has played a big part in the debate about minimum wage, and you can learn more about it with this resource from Johns Hopkins Medicine.

"How Kids Can Help the Homeless"
medium.com/@hccb/how-kids-can-help-homeless-8adca96a87dc
How can you help the homeless? Discover ideas from this article.

BOOKS

Brooks, Gene. *Poverty and Our Future*. New York, NY: PowerKids Press, 2022.

Brundle, Joanna. *Jobs*. New York, NY: KidHaven Publishing, 2019.

Hyde, Natalie. *Housing and Homelessness*. New York, NY: Crabtree Publishing Company, 2022.

INDEX